D0772817

GET TO KNOW
YOUR PET

Rabbits

JINNY JOHNSON

A+

Smart Apple Media

Smart Apple Media is published by Black Rabbit Books
P.O. Box 3263, Mankato, Minnesota 56002

Printed in the United States of America

Library of Congress Cataloging-in-Publication Data
Johnson, Jinny.
    Rabbits / Jinny Johnson.
        p. cm.—(Smart Apple Media. Get to know your pet)
    Includes index.
    Summary:"Describes the behavior of rabbits and how to choose and care for pet rabbits"—Provided by publisher.
        ISBN 978-1-59920-090-3
        1. Rabbits—Juvenile literature. I. Title.
SF453.2.J64 2009
636.932—dc22
                                                    2007043436

Designed by Guy Callaby
Edited by Mary-Jane Wilkins
Illustrations by Bill Donohoe
Picture research by Su Alexander

Thanks to Richard, James, Ella, Simon and Joe
for their help and advice.

Picture acknowledgements
Page 4 Neil McIntyre/Getty Images; 7 Jo Sax/Getty Images;
8 Herbert Kehrer/Zefa/Corbis; 11 Herbert Spichtinger/Zefa/
Corbis; 12 Catherine Ledner/Getty Images; 15 Roger Tidman/
Corbis; 17 Steve Shott/Getty Images; 18 Neo Vision/Getty Images;
20 Skip Brown/Getty Images; 23 Morton Beebe/Corbis; 24 Laurence
Monneret/Getty Images; 26 Susanne Borges/A.B./Zefa/Corbis
Front cover Ben Hall/Getty Images

9 8 7 6 5 4 3 2

Contents

Rabbits–Wild and Tame

Rabbits make loving family pets. They are gentle and good-tempered animals that need to be fed and have their cages cleaned out regularly. They also need plenty of exercise.

Wild rabbits are prey animals—they are hunted by predators such as foxes. This means they are nervous and shy. Pet rabbits are easily frightened and need kind, gentle treatment. They like company just as cats and dogs do.

Wild rabbits live in family groups, so a pet rabbit likes to have a friend to live with or lots of attention from you every day. A rabbit left on its own in a hutch, or cage, at the end of the yard will be very lonely and unhappy.

BUNNY FACT
Rabbits are not rodents like rats and mice. They belong to a group of mammals called lagomorphs. Hares and pikas are lagomorphs too.

Remember that rabbits are friendly, sociable animals in the wild, used to lots of company, and are not happy left by themselves.

4

PET SUBJECT

Q **Why does my rabbit twitch its nose all the time?**

A A rabbit twitches its nose to help it pick up every little smell. Rabbits have a very good sense of smell to help them watch out for predators in the wild. When your rabbit's nose is twitching fast, it can smell something that makes it frightened or excited. When its nose is twitching slowly, your rabbit is feeling calm and safe.

Rabbit Characteristics

- A rabbit has long ears and big, bulging eyes.

- Wild rabbits live in burrows and they have sharp claws on their front paws to help them dig holes in the ground.

- Rabbits eat only plant food. They have big front teeth for gathering their food.

- Rabbits live between seven and ten years.

A Rabbit's Day

Wild rabbits eat mainly grass. Rabbits love grass, but there's not a lot of nutrients in it.

To get enough nutrients from the grass they eat, wild rabbits need to spend most of the day feeding. Your pet rabbit will rely on you to give it food and fresh water every day.

PET SUBJECT

Q **Why do rabbits have such big ears?**

A A rabbit's long ears help it hear every sound, so it knows if danger is near. It can move each ear separately to hear sounds from different directions. It may be, though, that a rabbit has big ears to help it keep cool. If a rabbit is too hot, it lifts and opens up its ears to cool down.

Wild rabbits get plenty of exercise as they hop around looking for food. A pet rabbit needs exercise too, so you should let it out of its hutch every day, or give it a run large enough to move around in.

A rabbit also spends an hour or so every day grooming its fur. It licks itself clean and picks out any dirt or insects with its sharp teeth.

Rabbits need plenty of grass or hay to keep them fit and healthy.

Run, Freeze, or Fight

If a wild rabbit is in danger, it will try to run away, or stay very still and hope to avoid being noticed. If it has to, a rabbit will fight for its life, kicking with its strong back legs. Remember that your pet rabbit will also try to run away or kick if it is frightened.

Do Rabbits Talk?

Wild rabbits have signals to warn each other if a predator is near. Your pet rabbit doesn't need to worry about danger—it has you to look after it.

But it's a good idea to know the signs that show that your rabbit is feeling scared, worried, or happy. When a rabbit is scared, it crouches close to the ground and holds its ears flat on its back. If it shakes its ears around, it may be anxious or angry about something. But if your rabbit is lying on its side with its back legs stretched out, it is feeling happy and relaxed.

This wild rabbit looks frightened and is lying as close to the ground as it can—perhaps to escape the notice of a predator.

Rabbit Sounds

Rabbits are prey animals, so they don't make a lot of noise. That would attract the attention of predators. But they do make some sounds. You might hear your rabbit make gentle purring noises when it's feeling happy or little clicking sounds if it's just eaten a favorite treat. Rabbits can also growl and hiss if they are angry, and if you hear your rabbit grinding its teeth loudly, it might be in pain. A very frightened rabbit may scream loudly.

PET SUBJECT

Q **Why does my rabbit rub me with his chin?**

A When a rabbit rubs you—or anything else—with its chin, it is spreading its smell. As the rabbit rubs, an area under its chin releases a smelly substance. You'll probably hardly notice the scent of this, but the rabbit does and the smell makes it feel safe. Wild rabbits mark their territory in this way so other rabbits know they are there.

Rabbit Senses

A wild rabbit uses its senses of sight, smell, and hearing to stay safe and avoid dangerous predators.

Your pet rabbit has very good senses too. Look at your rabbit's bulgy eyes. They are on either side of its head, which means that the rabbit can see nearly everything around it. In fact, it's hardest for a rabbit to see what's right in front of it. However, even if it can't see something, it can hear or smell it.

Having eyes at the sides of its head helps a rabbit see any danger that might be creeping up behind.

PET SUBJECT

Q **Why does my rabbit keep looking up when he's eating?**

A When a wild rabbit is eating, it has to watch for danger. Every now and then it looks up, and may rear up on its back legs to take a good look around. Even though your pet rabbit is perfectly safe, it has the same feelings as a wild rabbit, so it keeps checking for danger.

Rubbing Noses

Rabbits greet each other by rubbing noses, and they lick and groom their friends. If your rabbit licks you and nuzzles you with its nose, it is a sign that it feels friendly toward you and likes your company. It shows that you are looking after your rabbit well and helping it feel happy and safe. Always wash your hands, though, after playing with your rabbit, and never kiss your pet.

Kinds of Rabbits

Pet rabbits come in many different sizes and colors. There are giant rabbits that you might struggle to lift and tiny dwarf rabbits.

There are long-haired rabbits and short-haired rabbits. There are even rabbits called lop ears, which have ears that hang down instead of standing up tall.

This is a lop ear rabbit. It can't lift up its long ears.

Long-haired rabbits such as angoras need brushing and combing every day.

Small or medium-sized rabbits are easier to care for than the giant types, which need lots of space. Long-haired rabbits need careful grooming so their fur doesn't become tangled and matted.

A female rabbit is called a doe and a male is a buck. Baby rabbits are called kittens.

Boy or Girl?

It's a good idea to have more than one rabbit, unless you can spend lots of time with your pet. Two females are best, or you can keep a male and female together if they have been neutered to prevent them from having young. Two males can only be kept together if they are neutered. If not, they will fight.

PET SUBJECT

Q **Why does my rabbit sometimes spray his pee?**

A It's usually male rabbits that do this, often when they are trying to be friendly with a female rabbit. But pet rabbits sometimes spray their owners, too—maybe they are just trying to say how much they like you. The best way to stop a rabbit from spraying is to have it neutered.

Choosing a Rabbit

You can buy rabbits from a pet store, though you may need to visit a breeder if you want a particular type. Best of all, give an unwanted rabbit a home and choose your pet at a rescue center.

What To Look For

Check your rabbit carefully before deciding to take it home. Look for these features.

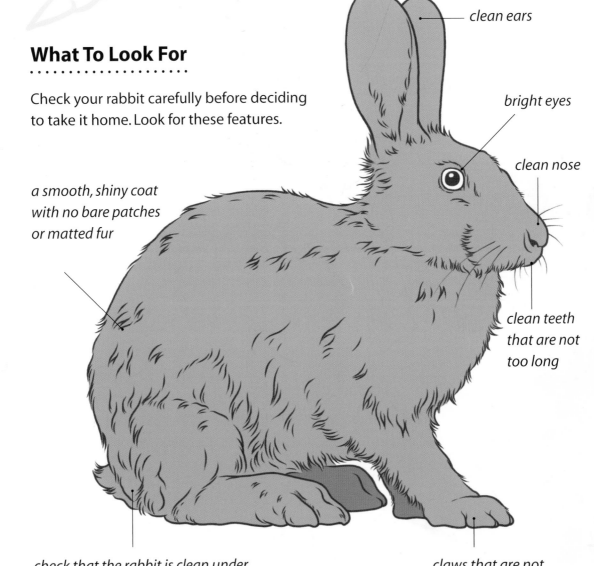

clean ears

bright eyes

clean nose

a smooth, shiny coat with no bare patches or matted fur

clean teeth that are not too long

check that the rabbit is clean under the tail, with no sign of runny poop

claws that are not torn or too long

A young rabbit is ready to leave its mother at around eight to twelve weeks old. If you are choosing from a litter of young rabbits, choose one that looks confident and not scared. Put your hand in the cage—rabbits that are used to people won't be frightened or try to bite. They might even come and give you a sniff!

PET SUBJECT

Q **Why does my rabbit try to dig up the carpet?**

A All rabbits are burrowers. In the wild, rabbits dig underground burrows with their strong claws. This is what your bunny is trying to do.

To stop it from trying to burrow in the carpet, you could give your rabbit plenty of hay to dig in inside its hutch or give it a cardboard box filled with newspaper. You could also give your rabbit a sandbox to dig in.

What Your Rabbit Needs

A pet rabbit needs quite a few things to be comfortable. A rabbit may live for ten years, so it's worth buying the best you can afford.

A hutch or cage is the most important item—buy one as large as possible and which is easy to clean. You'll need bedding, a drip-feed water bottle, food bowls, rabbit food, and a grooming brush. A hutch for two medium-sized rabbits should measure at least 71 x 35 x 30 inches (180 x 90 x 75 cm). It should have an area with a wire mesh front where the rabbit can feed and exercise. It also needs a sleeping area with a solid front where the rabbit can sleep as though in a dark, cozy burrow.

Buy a big rabbit hutch for your pets. The more room your rabbits have, the happier and healthier they will be.

Make sure the hutch is sturdy enough to keep your rabbits warm and dry and is raised off the ground on legs or bricks. A hutch on the ground will be damp and cold. Put the hutch in a sheltered spot away from the wind and full sun.

Indoor Home

If you want to keep your rabbit indoors, buy a cage with a plastic base and wire top. Never keep a rabbit in a cage with a wire base, as this will hurt its tender feet. Put the cage where it is not in full sun or drafts. Rabbits like a nesting box too, where they can snuggle down when they want peace and quiet.

Indoor cages are fine, too, but make sure you let your rabbits out every day.

17

PET SUBJECT

Q Why do rabbits have big back legs?

A A rabbit's back legs are stronger than its front legs. They help the rabbit hop along and sit up to see what's happening around it. Strong back legs allow a rabbit to jump and twist around quickly if it is being chased.

Bringing Your Rabbit Home

The first few days in a new home can be difficult. Baby rabbits will miss their mother and feel a bit frightened until they grow used to you. A grown-up rabbit needs time to feel at home too.

Baby rabbits are born blind and helpless, with no fur. A couple of weeks later their eyes are open and they have a fluffy coat.

Line the floor of the rabbit's hutch or cage with newspaper. Add a layer of wood shavings and some hay in the sleeping area.

Be gentle with your new pet or pets. Speak quietly and don't try to handle them too much at first. Leave them alone to get used to their new home for the first day. Then sit on the floor and let the rabbits come to you. Stroke your rabbits and reward them with a treat.

BUNNY FACT
Rabbits can jump up to 3.3 feet (1 m) high.

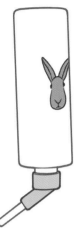

Cleaning Out the Hutch

Rabbits are naturally clean, but when they live in a cage, they need some help from you to keep it clean.

Every Day
- Wash and dry food bowls
- Wash and refill water bottle
- Check litter tray and/or sweep out droppings

Every Few Days
- Check bedding and take out any that is dirty or wet
- Clean litter tray and refill or sweep out droppings

Every Week
- Clean hutch, remove all bedding, hay, and newspaper, and provide clean bedding. If your rabbit lives in a plastic indoor cage, wash the base every week.

Every Month
- Wash and disinfect the inside of the hutch and allow it to dry completely before putting in new bedding.

PET SUBJECT

Q Why does my bunny thump his back foot?

A Wild rabbits do this to tell others that danger is near—perhaps a predator. The sound can be heard by other rabbits above ground and those down in their burrows. A pet rabbit will thump if it's frightened or thinks that something is coming into its home.

Feeding Your Rabbit

Rabbits are plant-eaters and do not eat meat. About three-quarters of your rabbit's diet should be hay.

A pet rabbit must always have fresh hay. Fit a hayrack to the rabbit's cage or hutch to keep the hay clean and dry. Pet rabbits also need rabbit mix or cereal (from a pet store) and raw vegetables. Give new fresh foods one at a time so you'll know if anything upsets your rabbit. Never give rabbits chips, cake, or chocolate.

Give your rabbit dried food every morning and fresh food in the evening. Rabbits need fresh water and hay at all times. Every day, take out any fresh food your rabbit hasn't eaten and wash the food bowls.

Wild rabbits eat leaves, plant roots, buds, and even tree bark.

Fresh Foods

Wash fresh food and give your rabbit a good variety. Favorites include cabbage, carrots, cauliflower leaves, celery, kale, peas and peapods, Brussels sprouts, apples, pears, and broccoli. Your rabbit will also enjoy fresh grass and plants such as comfrey, shepherd's purse, chickweed, dandelion, or clover. Check that any grass and weeds you pick haven't been sprayed with weedkiller or fertilizer. **Don't give green vegetables to rabbits under 12 weeks old.**

PET SUBJECT

Q Why does my rabbit sometimes eat his poop?

A This is normal. Wild rabbits eat mostly grass, which is hard for an animal's body to break down. The little soft droppings that a rabbit eats are partly-digested food. The rabbit eats them so the food goes through its body again and is broken down further. The little hard, dry droppings you see are what the rabbit can't use.

House Rabbits

Rabbits don't have to live in hutches. Some people allow their rabbits to run around indoors. Your rabbit will enjoy your company and get plenty of exercise.

You need to train a house rabbit to use a litter box. Make sure that it has a cage to sleep in at night and to keep it safe when you're not around. House rabbits should be neutered.

House rabbits need to spend time outside too, so you'll need an outdoor run where your pet is safe from cats and dogs. You can even train your rabbit to wear a harness and take it for a walk on a leash.

Rabbit-Proofing

Rabbits like to chew, so watch out for electric wires, furniture, carpets, and houseplants. Try keeping your rabbit to a couple of rooms where it is safe—and give it plenty of toys to chew.

House rabbits and cats can become good friends. But introduce them slowly and carefully and keep an eye on them until you are sure they are happy together.

PET SUBJECT

Q **Why do rabbits like to chew?**

A A rabbit's teeth grow all through its life, to allow it to keep chewing the tough food it eats. If a pet rabbit doesn't chew enough, its teeth grow too long. Give it something hard to chew, such as a piece of apple wood or a toy from the pet store. This should prevent its teeth from growing too long and will give your rabbit something to do.

Training and Play

Rabbits can be trained to sit up and beg for a favorite treat. They can also learn to understand when you say "no" and to use a litter box.

The best way to teach a rabbit is by reward. If you want your rabbit to sit up and beg, offer it a treat, but hold it so the rabbit has to sit up to reach. As it does so, say "sit up."

If you repeat this often enough, the rabbit will learn what to do and sit up when it sees your hand raised—even without the food. Only give tiny treats, so your rabbit doesn't get fat, and make sure they are healthy foods.

Offer a healthy treat such as a piece of carrot to encourage your rabbit to sit up when you ask it to.

Using a Litter Box

If you let your rabbit roam the house you need to teach it to use a litter box. If the rabbit uses a box in its hutch, it makes cleaning it out easier. Use a small cat litter box and some wood-based cat litter or wood shavings. Clay-based or clumping litter is dangerous for rabbits. Put some droppings in the box and perhaps a piece of paper towel with some of the rabbit's pee. Your rabbit will soon get the idea.

There are bound to be accidents at first, but your rabbit will soon get used to using a litter box.

PET SUBJECT

Q Do rabbits like to play?

A You see wild rabbits chasing each other for fun. Pet rabbits like to play too. Rabbits enjoy cardboard tube tunnels or boxes with holes they can run through in the side. They will also throw small things such as pinecones and toilet paper tubes around. Another idea is to hide small pieces of food in a toy such as a willow ball so your pet can have fun finding them.

Holding and Handling

Rabbits are easily frightened, so handle your pet gently. Let a rabbit get used to its new home for a few days. Then stroke it every day so it comes to know and trust you.

Never grab your rabbit or speak loudly while you're holding it. And never pick up a rabbit by its ears. That hurts! Rabbits are easily injured if they fall or are dropped, so be very careful when holding your rabbit.

Picking Up a Rabbit

When you pick up your rabbit, hold the scruff of the neck with one hand and put your other hand underneath its back legs. Keep it close to you so it feels safe. When you put your rabbit back in its hutch, lower it in back feet first in case it gets frightened and kicks out at you. A rabbit's back legs are strong and a kick could hurt you. Rabbits like routine so try to feed and play with your pet at the same time every day.

PET SUBJECT

Q Why do even dark-colored bunnies have tails that are white or light-colored underneath?

A For wild rabbits, the white tail acts as a warning to others. If a rabbit is escaping from danger, it holds up its tail so others will see the flash of white and know that something is up. The light tail helps rabbits see each other while they are feeding too.

Grooming your rabbit is a good way to get to know each other. Rabbits don't much like being picked up. It's better to sit on the floor with your rabbit and brush or stroke it gently.

While you are grooming, look out for fleas, sores, or wounds that might need attention.

For Parents and Caregivers

Caring for any pet is a big responsibility. Looking after an animal takes time and money, and children cannot do everything themselves. You'll need to show them how to behave around the animal, provide what it needs, and make sure it is healthy and has the necessary vaccinations.

A rabbit may live for ten years, so owning one is a big commitment. But helping to look after a pet and learning to respect it and handle it gently is good for children and can be great fun.

CHOOSING A RABBIT

Make sure you choose a healthy animal. If you buy a rabbit from a pet store, take it to the vet for a checkup and vaccinations against myxomatosis and VHD (Viral Hemorrhagic Disease). Ask the vet to check the sex of the animal. Pet stores sometimes get it wrong!

If you find your pet at a rescue center, it will probably have been vaccinated and neutered. Be prepared for the rescue center to ask you questions about your life and your home. Don't be offended—they are trying to do the best for their animals and to make sure that you have a pet that suits you.

Once you've chosen your pet, you'll need a carrying cage or a sturdy cardboard box to bring it home in. A cat carrier is fine, or use a carrying box if your vet can supply one.

HOUSING

You'll need to organize a hutch or cage and run for your rabbit, which can be expensive. You'll also need to help your child clean out the hutch regularly. A rabbit's cage gets dirty very quickly and it is important to keep it clean or the rabbit may get ill.

FEEDING

Once a rabbit is settled, a child can give it dry food and change its water daily. Your children can give the rabbit fresh food too, but make sure they know what is safe for the animal to eat. It is best to give your pet dried food pellets, rather than mixed flakes. Some rabbits just pick out the bits they like from the mixes and don't eat a balanced diet.

HANDLING

It's important to show your child how to handle a rabbit properly and teach children that it is not a cuddly toy. If a child handles a rabbit roughly, it will be nervous and insecure and unlikely to be a loving pet.

Teach your child to respect animals and treat them gently. Don't let a child grab the rabbit and speak loudly, especially at first when the animal will be anxious. Make sure you stroke and handle your pet every day. Rabbits can become wild very quickly if not handled regularly.

HEALTH CHECK

Keep an eye on your rabbit's health and watch for signs of illness. Check regularly for signs of parasites. You also need to make sure that the rabbit's claws and teeth don't grow too long. Take it to the vet if its claws need clipping.

Rabbits sometimes have orange- or red-colored urine. This may happen in cold weather, if the rabbit has been given antibiotics, or if it has eaten lots of carrots. This is nothing to worry about, but if the rabbit's urine is very dark, it can mean that it is not drinking enough water.

NEUTERING

Pet rabbits should be neutered, especially if you want a rabbit to have the run of the house.

Glossary

breeder
Someone who keeps pedigree rabbits and sells the young they produce.

burrow
A hole dug in the ground where a wild rabbit makes its home and cares for its young.

grooming
Caring for and cleaning the fur. You can groom your rabbit by brushing or combing its fur.

hutch
A home for a pet rabbit. A hutch is usually made of wood and kept outside.

lop ears
Lop ears are very long ears which hang down instead of being held up. There are several breeds of lop-eared rabbits.

myxomatosis
An infectious illness suffered by rabbits. Your pet rabbit can be vaccinated so it does not catch myxomatosis.

neutering
An operation performed by a vet on an animal so that it cannot have babies.

parasites
Tiny creatures such as fleas, lice, and mites, which can live on a rabbit's body.

predator
An animal that kills and eats other animals.

prey
Animals that are hunted and eaten by other animals.

scruff
The loose skin at the back of the neck.

vaccination
An injection given to your rabbit by the vet to prevent it from catching certain serious illnesses.

VHD (Viral Hemorrhagic Disease)
An infectious illness suffered by rabbits. Your pet rabbit can be vaccinated so it does not catch VHD.

Web Sites

For Kids:

ASPCA Animaland: Pet Care
http://www.aspca.org/site/PageServer?pagename=kids_pc_rabbit_411
The American Society for the Prevention of Cruelty to Animals has some excellent advice about caring for your pets.

Animed: Pet Care Information Tips
http://www.animed.org/rabbits.htm
Animed offers articles covering how to know if a rabbit is right for you, common health problems, nutritional needs, and much more about rabbits.

Precious Pet Rabbits
http://www.pet-rabbit-care-information.com/
A veteran rabbit breeder shares information about rabbit pet care, breeding, and more.

Rabbit, Horse, and Other Pet Care
http://www.hsus.org/pets/pet_care/rabbit_horse_and_other_pet_care/
The Humane Society of the United States offers rabbit care essentials, including housing, diet, litter box training, and much more.

For Teachers:

Best Friends Animal Society: Humane Education Classroom Resources
http://www.bestfriends.org/atthesanctuary/humaneeducation/classroomresources.cfm
Lesson plans and lots of information about treating animals humanely.

Education World Lesson Plans: Pet Week Lessons for Every Grade
http://www.educationworld.com/a_lesson/lesson/lesson311.shtml
Use the topic of pets to engage your students in math, language arts, life science, and art.

Lesson Plans: Responsible Pet Care
http://www.kindnews.org/teacher_zone/lesson_plans.asp
Lesson plans for grades preschool through sixth, covering language arts, social studies, math, science, and health.

Index